The Only Marketing

Discover the path of authenticity in a universe of imitations.

Copyright

Summary:

- *a brief introduction*
- *The story behind the concept*
- *The 2 types of mechanism*
- *She is everywhere*
- *The mechanism of the problem*
- *The solution mechanism*
- *The role of creativity in the implementation of the mechanism*
- *6 hats technique*
- *Connecting people to the unique mechanism*
- *Connecting the 2 mechanisms*
- *the perfect structure*
- *Conclusion*

a brief introduction

You may have already noticed that the market is increasingly competitive and that it is necessary to stand out to be noticed by customers and succeed in business. One of the best ways to differentiate yourself from the competition (perhaps the only one) is through the unique engine.

The marketing strategy that seeks to make the brand unique and admired, awakening a desire for mystery in customers and potential customers.

It's like the company has a secret that no one else has and that makes people feel attracted to the brand and want to know more about it.

To create a unique mechanism, it is necessary to identify what makes the brand special and different from others. It could be a unique product, an inspiring story, a different philosophy or exceptional service. The important thing is that this differential is valued by customers and generates an emotional connection with the brand.

By using the single engine as a marketing strategy, the company can realize several benefits, such as increased customer engagement, increased brand loyalty and increased sales. In addition, the brand becomes more relevant in the market and can consolidate itself as a reference in its segment.

So if you want to stand out from the competition and be a unique and admired brand, start thinking about how you can create a unique engine for your business. Identify what makes you special and value that differential. Sure enough, that's what you'll find here.

The story behind the concept

The single engine is a strategic approach that is increasingly being adopted by companies around the world.

This approach consists of creating a single, coherent message that is conveyed across all marketing channels in order to create a consistent brand image and strengthen the target audience's perception of the company.

But how did the idea for this unique marketing engine come about?

To better understand this concept, you need to go back a few decades in time and observe how marketing has evolved over the years.

In the early days of marketing, the approach was simpler and more straightforward. Companies focused on producing quality products or services and selling them to as many customers as possible. Advertising campaigns were created with the aim of informing consumers about the products or services available, highlighting their features and benefits.

Over time, companies realized that this approach was not enough to stand out in an increasingly competitive market. Then came the first attempts to create a brand image that was more than just a name or a logo. Companies began to invest in more elaborate advertising campaigns that appealed to consumers' emotions and feelings.

But it wasn't until the 1980s that the idea of the single marketing engine emerged, which was popularized by authors such as Al Ries and Jack Trout. This approach was inspired by the idea that companies should focus on a single, coherent message rather than trying to convey several different messages at once.

The concept of a single marketing mechanism is based on the idea that companies should identify a single benefit or feature of their products or services that is really meaningful to consumers. This feature must be emphasized in all marketing campaigns, regardless of the communication channel used.

The objective of the unique marketing mechanism is to create a strong and coherent brand image that is easily recognized by the target audience. This approach takes into account the fact that consumers are bombarded with a myriad of marketing messages every day. If a company tries to convey several different messages at the same time, it risks confusing consumers and diluting brand awareness.

On the other hand, if a company focuses on a single message that is truly meaningful to consumers, it is more likely to create a strong and coherent brand image. This message must be emphasized in all communication channels used by the company, from traditional advertising to social networks and content marketing.

To exemplify this idea, we can think of companies like Apple. The Apple brand is recognized around the world for its unique message of innovation and design. This message is emphasized in all of the company's marketing campaigns, from television commercials to product pages on its website. As a result, Apple has managed to create a strong and coherent brand image that is recognized around the world.

The way people see the world and interpret the information they receive is influenced by many factors, such as their life experiences, skills, knowledge, values and beliefs. These factors contribute to shaping each individual's perspective, which in turn leads to different ways of seeing the same solution.

For example, suppose a team of professionals is called in to solve a problem in a company. Each team member will bring their own perspective based on their background, experiences and skills. Some team members may be more analytical and detail oriented, while others may be more creative and think of innovative solutions. Some may have a broader view of the problem, while others may have a more focused view of specific aspects.

Furthermore, a person's emotions and emotional state can also influence their perception and interpretation of a solution. If someone is going through a difficult time or is stressed, it may be harder for them to see alternative solutions or be open-minded to different approaches. Likewise, someone who is feeling confident and motivated may be more likely to consider creative and innovative solutions.

Differences in perspective can lead to heated discussions and even conflicts in a work group. However, it's important to remember that these differences can be valuable as they allow the team to see the problem from different angles and therefore arrive at more comprehensive and effective solutions. When people work together, it's important to recognize and value these differences, rather than trying to suppress them.

Another factor that can influence how people view a solution is culture. A person's culture can influence their beliefs and values, which in turn can affect their perception of a solution. For example, in some cultures, creativity is valued, while in others, compliance is more important. These cultural differences can lead to different approaches to solving problems.

Furthermore, the way information is presented can also influence the way people view a solution. If information is presented clearly and concisely, it will be easier for people to understand the problem and possible solutions. On the other hand, if the information is presented in a confusing or disorganized way, it can make it difficult to understand the problem and identify solutions.

Differences in perspective can also be influenced by a person's experience in a particular field. For example, an engineer might have a different perspective on a problem than a marketing expert. These differences can lead to different approaches to solving a problem and to more innovative and creative solutions.

It is important to remember that differences in perspective are not necessarily an obstacle to finding effective solutions, but rather an opportunity to enhance creativity and collaboration within a group. When people share their perspectives openly and respectfully, it can lead to healthy discussion and a more comprehensive approach to the issue. Sometimes the most creative solutions are found by combining different ideas and perspectives.

It is worth remembering that, in certain cases, differences in perspective can be an obstacle to effective decision-making. This can occur when people have very different values and beliefs or when their perspectives are so divergent that they cannot agree. In these cases, it may be necessary to seek out a mediator or third party who can help find a common path.

To minimize differences in perspective, it's important for people to be clear about their goals and expectations. This can help ensure that everyone is on the same page and working towards the same goals. It is also important that all team members have access to the same information and have the opportunity to voice their opinions.

In summary, differences in perspective are a reality in any group or team, and can be valuable in the search for innovative and effective solutions. However, it is important to remember that these differences can also lead to conflict and that effort is needed to ensure that all team members are working together towards a common goal. By recognizing and valuing these differences, we can leverage the diversity of perspectives to find more creative and effective solutions to the challenges we face.

The 2 types of mechanism

The concept of a single problem and solution mechanism emerged from the need for companies to stand out in an increasingly competitive and saturated market. Companies realized that they needed to create a more effective marketing strategy that was capable of attracting public attention and creating a competitive edge.

The idea behind the single engine is quite simple: identify a common target audience problem and provide a unique and innovative solution to that problem.

The strategy focuses on finding a problem that the target audience faces on a daily basis that has not yet been satisfactorily resolved by other companies. From there, the company creates a unique solution that solves the problem effectively and efficiently.

The single engine concept was popularized by Donald Miller, author of "Building a StoryBrand: Clarify Your Message So Customers Will Listen". According to Miller, most companies fail to capture the public's attention because they fail to communicate clearly and effectively. He argues that companies need to be able to communicate their message clearly and simply so that the public understands what problem the company solves and how it solves that problem.

To implement the single mechanism of problem and solution, the company needs to follow some steps. First of all, it is necessary to identify the problem that the target audience faces. For this, it is important to carry out market research and talk to the public to understand what their challenges and frustrations are. It is necessary to understand the problem in a deep and detailed way, so that the solution created is really effective and relevant.

Once the problem is identified, the company needs to create a unique and innovative solution to this problem. The solution must be able to solve the problem effectively and efficiently, and it must stand out from the solutions offered by other companies. It's important that the solution is easy to understand and use so that the audience immediately understands how it can solve their problem.

To communicate the unique engine effectively, the company needs to create a clear and simple message that highlights the unique solution it offers. The message should communicate what problem the company solves and how it solves that problem. It is important that the message is easy to understand and memorize, so that the public will remember the company when they need to solve the problem at hand.

The unique problem and solution mechanism can be applied to different industries. Tech companies, for example, can identify common user problems and create unique solutions that improve the user experience. Retail companies can identify common customer issues and create unique solutions that make the shopping experience more enjoyable and convenient.

By implementing the unique mechanism of problem and solution, companies are able to stand out in a competitive market and create a competitive edge. The strategy allows companies to clearly and effectively communicate how they can solve a specific target audience problem, making it the obvious choice.

She is everywhere

There is no way you can find the unique mechanism without it...

THE SEARCH!

Fundamental in all aspects of marketing, from identifying target audiences to creating effective marketing messages. When it comes to finding your product or service's unique engine, research is special.

It may involve several steps such as sales data analysis, competitor analysis, interviewing potential customers and market research. By conducting this research, you can identify market trends and needs and determine how your product or service can uniquely meet those needs.

For example, if you are creating a new cosmetics brand, you can conduct market research to find out what common issues people face with their skin and what they are looking for in a skin care product. Based on this information, you can identify a unique problem mechanism that your product can solve, such as reducing skin redness or intense hydration.

Research can also help you identify gaps in the market that your product or service can fill. For example, if you notice that many skin care products are targeted towards women and there are few options for men, you can create a unique solution engine that specifically addresses the needs of men.

When conducting research, it is important to be objective and unbiased, and not let your personal assumptions influence your results. Analyze the data carefully and be willing to listen to negative feedback or constructive criticism. This can help you identify issues you may not have previously considered and find more effective solutions.

Also remember that research is not a one-time job. As your market and your business evolve, it's important to continue to conduct research to ensure you're up to date on market needs and industry trends. This can help you identify new opportunities for business growth and maintain your competitive edge.

In short, the unique marketing engine is an effective approach to stand out from the competition and attract potential customers. However, identifying this unique mechanism is not an easy task. You need to conduct extensive research to identify market trends and needs and determine how your product or service can uniquely meet those needs. By doing this, you can create an effective marketing strategy that builds your brand and attracts potential customers to your business.

The mechanism of the problem

Imagine a man on a beach, looking at the horizon while waiting for a big wave that is about to break. He knows the wave is coming and it's going to engulf him, but he doesn't know exactly how to prepare for it.

This scene can be seen as an analogy for the mechanism of the problem in marketing. The man represents the company or the entrepreneur, who knows there is a problem looming but doesn't yet know how to deal with it. The wave represents the problem, which could be a change in the market, new competition, or new customer demand.

Just like the man on the beach, the company needs to be prepared to face the problem that is coming. It is necessary to have adequate strategies and tools to deal with change and find creative solutions to overcome the problem.

Starting with the mechanism of the problem is the key step to finding efficient and satisfying solutions for your target audience. To do this, you need to go beyond superficial issues and delve into the problems your audience faces.

To begin with, it's important to ask the right questions to understand what all the problems your prospect is facing and how the lack of your solution could affect them. It is also necessary to analyze the solutions that he has already found and why they are not effective in solving the problem in question.

By finding a pattern in the answers, it is possible to identify a possible symptom and, from there, seek the root of the problem. It's important to remember that there are no shortcuts to this process, and it takes dedicated and persistent work to find the unique engine that will make a difference for your audience.

If you realize that the solutions your prospect has already tried do not reach the root of the problem, you are one step away from finding the ideal solution. By understanding what is blocking your prospect from achieving the desired results, you can create a solution that effectively meets their needs.

Don't settle for superficial and generic solutions. By digging deeper into your target audience's problems and finding the unique mechanism that will make a difference, you can offer a solution that really makes a difference and earns your customers' trust and loyalty.

Focus on identifying and solving a specific problem for your target audience. It is an approach that aims to provide a unique solution to a problem that many people are facing, in order to make the brand or product stand out in the market.

The idea is that, by presenting an innovative and effective solution to a common problem, the company can attract the attention and loyalty of consumers, generating more sales and profit.

Here are some practical examples of how companies can use the unique mechanism of the problem in their digital marketing strategy:

Dollar Shave Club

Dollar Shave Club is a razor blade subscription company that focuses on solving a common problem: the frequent and expensive purchase of razor blades. Instead of having customers go to the store to buy the blades, Dollar Shave Club **offers monthly home delivery of blades for a fixed fee.**

The company created a viral video in which CEO Michael Dubin explains the company's value proposition in a funny and irreverent way. The video attracted millions of views and helped the company grow rapidly.

Uber

Uber is a transportation app that solves the problem of finding a reliable taxi or public transport. With Uber, you can order a private car with just a few clicks on your phone.

The company used the problem's unique mechanism to stand out in the transportation market. Uber recognized that many people were having trouble finding reliable transportation and came up with an innovative solution to solve this problem.

Dropbox

Dropbox is a cloud storage company that focuses on solving the data storage problem. Many people face the problem of not having enough space to store their files on their devices.

Dropbox solves this problem by offering a cloud storage service, allowing people to store their files in a safe place and access them from anywhere in the world.

Netflix

Netflix is a video streaming company that solves the problem of finding quality content to watch. Before the emergence of

Netflix, many people faced the problem of not having easy access to quality movies and TV series.

Netflix has solved this problem by creating a video streaming platform that offers a wide variety of high quality content to watch anytime, anywhere.

Amazon

Amazon is an e-commerce company that focuses on solving the problem of finding and buying products quickly and conveniently. Before Amazon, many people faced the problem of having to go to the physical store to buy products.

Amazon solved this problem by creating an easy-to-use e-commerce platform that allows customers to buy products in just a few clicks and have them delivered to their doorstep.

The single problem engine, in short, is a marketing approach that focuses on identifying and presenting a single, specific problem that your product or service can uniquely and effectively solve. The idea is that by clearly identifying and communicating the problem your product or service solves, you can differentiate yourself from the competition and increase the likelihood of attracting potential customers.

The solution mechanism

Defining the solution engine is the next critical step after identifying the root problem your audience faces.

From that point on, it is necessary to create a solution that directly attacks the problem in an effective way and that makes it very evident how its mechanism "cuts the problem at the root".

To define the mechanism of the solution, it is necessary to answer some important questions. First, you need to explain why your solution is better than others available on the market. For this, it is necessary to highlight the differentials and advantages that it offers in relation to the other options.

Another important question is what your solution specifically addresses at the root of the problem. You need to clearly and objectively explain how your solution effectively solves the problem and why it is the best option for your target audience.

An important exercise in developing a clear and concise explanation of the effectiveness of your solution is to answer the question:why was the customer not successful with known solutions and how will your solution ensure customer success?

It is important to highlight the weaknesses of the solutions available on the market and explain how your solution differentiates itself by directly attacking the root of the problem. It is necessary to show how your solution presents a unique mechanism that really makes a difference in solving the problem your audience faces.

In addition, it is important to offer examples and real success stories of customers who used your solution and obtained effective results. This helps strengthen the credibility of your solution and build trust with your target audience.

Another important point in defining the solution mechanism is the simplicity and clarity of the explanation. It is necessary to avoid complex technical terms or confusing explanations that could make it difficult for the public to understand. The explanation needs to be clear, objective and easy to understand so that the target audience can understand the effectiveness of your solution and feel confident in using it.

Finally, remember that defining the solution mechanism is an ongoing process that may require adjustments and adaptations over time. It is necessary to always be aware of the needs and demands of the target audience and constantly seek to improve the solution to ensure its effectiveness and relevance in the market.

Defining the solution mechanism is a fundamental step for the success of any enterprise. By creating a solution that directly attacks the root of your target audience's problem, you can stand out in the market and gain customer loyalty and trust. Therefore, it is important to invest time and dedication in this process and always seek to offer increasingly effective and relevant solutions.

The role of creativity in the implementation of the mechanism

The unique marketing engine is a strategic approach that aims to make a company stand out in the market through a unique and clear value proposition. This value proposition is what differentiates a company from others, making it more attractive to its customers and potential customers.

However, to implement this approach successfully, it is essential to have a key element: creativity. Creativity is key to creating a unique value proposition and finding innovative ways to present it to your target audience.

Creativity in defining the unique value proposition

A company's unique value proposition is what makes it unique and different from others. It is a concise statement that describes the value the company provides to its customers and how it differentiates itself from competitors.

To define a unique value proposition, one must have a deep understanding of the target audience, their needs, desires and challenges. You need to think about how the company can satisfy these needs in a way that no other company can.

In this process of defining the value proposition, creativity is essential to find innovative and differentiated solutions.

Creativity can help a company think outside the box and find ways to satisfy customer needs in a way that competitors are not.

For example, if a company operates in the natural products market, the unique value proposition may be to offer a wide variety of organic and sustainable products, which is already a differentiator in the market. However, if this company uses creativity, it can create a differentiated experience for its customers, such as a store with nature-themed decor, events and workshops to promote a healthier lifestyle, among other innovative ideas.

Creativity in presenting the unique value proposition

In addition to defining the value proposition, creativity is also important in how it is presented to the target audience. A unique value proposition can be amazing, but if it's not presented in a compelling and engaging way, it won't have the desired impact.

Creativity can help a company find ways to present its unique value proposition clearly and impactfully across different marketing channels. For example, the company might create an ad campaign with an emotional video that tells the brand's story and highlights the unique value proposition.

Another idea would be to create a blog or podcast that addresses topics that are relevant to the target audience and that are aligned with the company's unique value proposition. This will help the company build authority in the market and attract more customers.

Creativity can also be applied in creating content for social networks, such as posts, images and videos. It's important that the content is creative and relevant to the target audience, and that it aligns with the company's unique value proposition.

Creativity in problem solving

One of the hallmarks of creativity is the ability to find solutions to complex and challenging problems. And in the world of marketing, this skill is essential to successfully implement the unique engine.

Throughout the implementation of the single mechanism, the company is likely to face challenges and obstacles. These challenges can include a lack of resources, fierce competition, or even sudden changes in the market. In these moments, creativity can be the key to finding innovative solutions and overcoming these obstacles.

For example, if the company is facing difficulties to stand out in the market, creativity can help to find new marketing channels or communication strategies that have not yet been explored by competitors. The company can use creativity to come up with a different approach to reach its target audience.

Furthermore, creativity can also be used to enhance already implemented marketing strategies. The company can experiment with new approaches, test different marketing channels and create innovative content to more effectively engage the target audience.

Creativity can also help the company adapt to market changes. In an ever-evolving market, it is essential that companies are willing to adapt and change their approach according to market needs. And creativity can be the key to finding new solutions and ideas that help the company remain relevant and competitive.

Marketing's unique engine is a strategic approach that can help companies stand out in the market and attract more customers. However, to implement it successfully, creativity is essential.

Companies that incorporate creativity into their marketing approach are more likely to find innovative solutions and create a unique experience for their customers. And that can make all the difference in the company's success and longevity in the market.

Creativity is key to creating the unique mechanism in a marketing strategy. Here are some techniques that can help spark your creativity and find innovative solutions:

Brainstorming: This technique involves generating ideas as a group, without judgment or criticism. The objective is to generate as many ideas as possible in a short period of time, which will later be analyzed to select the best ones. Brainstorming can be done as a team or individually.

Mind map: This technique involves creating a visual map of ideas and concepts that connect to each other. Mind mapping can help organize ideas and find new connections and creative solutions.

Lateral thinking: This technique involves a non-linear and unusual approach to problem solving. Rather than following a logical and traditional line of thinking, lateral thinking encourages the search for unexpected and creative solutions.

Analogies: The analogy technique involves comparing seemingly different ideas and concepts, looking for similarities and possible creative solutions. This technique can help you think outside the box and find new perspectives.

Observation and research: To find creative solutions, it is important to observe the market, target audience and competition. Research and observation can provide valuable insights that can be used in creating the unique engine.

These are just a few techniques that can help spark creativity in creating the unique mechanism in a marketing strategy. It's important to remember that everyone has a different creative process, and that you need to experiment with different techniques until you find what works best for you.

6 hats technique

The Six Hats Technique was created by writer and consultant Edward de Bono to help people think more creatively and effectively in groups. The technique involves wearing six different "mind hats," each representing a different way of thinking and approaching the problem at hand.

Each of the six hats represents a different way of thinking:

White hat: represents objective and factual information, the facts and figures that help to support ideas and make decisions rationally.

Red hat: represents intuition, emotions and personal reactions to the problem in question. It's time to express feelings, intuitions and guesses.

Black hat: represents critical judgment and negative evaluation of ideas, arguments and proposed solutions. It is time to analyze weaknesses and gaps in logic.

Yellow hat: represents optimism, positive evaluation and recognition of proposed ideas and solutions. It is time to value strengths and opportunities.

Green hat: represents creativity and the generation of new and innovative ideas. It's time to think outside the box, explore new possibilities and find unusual solutions.

Blue hat: represents the overview, process management and organization of proposed ideas and solutions. It is time to evaluate the effectiveness of the proposed strategies and to think about the next step.

The idea of the technique is that, by using each of these hats separately and systematically, participants are able to explore the problem in question more fully and efficiently, evaluating it from different angles and finding more creative and innovative solutions.

The Six Hats Technique can be used in different situations, such as in team meetings, in the elaboration of projects and marketing strategies, in the development of new products or services, among others. To use the technique, it is important to establish clear rules for its application, such as defining the time for each step, respecting each participant's turn and avoiding premature criticism and judgments.

Connecting people to the unique mechanism

The unique mechanism is a marketing approach that aims to identify and highlight the uniqueness of a product or service in relation to its competitors. However, it is important to highlight that this uniqueness is only possible thanks to the presence and influence of people in the process of creating and using the products.

People are the center of the unique mechanism, as they are the ones who identify the problems that need to be solved and seek solutions that meet their needs and desires. They are also the ones who evaluate and compare the options available on the market and decide which product or service is the most suitable for their demands.

In addition, people are also responsible for contributing ideas and feedback that help to improve and perfect the products and services offered. From this information, companies can identify the strengths and weaknesses of their products, as well as opportunities for improvement and innovation.

It is important to highlight that the single mechanism is not a single and definitive strategy, but rather a continuous process of improvement and improvement. Companies need to be constantly attentive to the demands and expectations of consumers in order to identify new opportunities for development and innovation.

It is essential that companies invest in market research and data analysis to understand the needs and desires of their consumers. From this information, it is possible to develop products and services that meet the demands of the target audience, making them unique in relation to their competitors.

However, the creation of a single mechanism should not be seen as an isolated process restricted to companies. People also have an important role to play in this process, since they are the ones who identify the needs and problems that need to be solved.

Companies must be open to listening and considering their customers' opinions and feedback in order to improve and perfect their products and services. In addition, companies can also encourage the active participation of consumers in the creation and development of new products, through opinion surveys and discussion groups.

In summary, the single mechanism only exists because of people, as they are the ones who identify the needs and problems that need to be solved, as well as the solutions that best meet their demands. Companies need to be constantly aware of the needs and expectations of their target audience in order to develop products and services that are unique and differentiated from their competitors.

Therefore, it is important for companies to invest in market research and data analysis in order to understand the needs and desires of consumers. In addition, companies must also be open to listening and considering their customers' feedbacks and opinions in order to improve and perfect their products and services. Only in this way is it possible to create a unique mechanism that is truly efficient and effective.

Connecting the 2 mechanisms

The unique mechanism of the solution is the key to solving a specific problem, but its existence is directly related to the unique mechanism of the problem in question. In other words, it is impossible to have a unique and effective solution without deeply understanding the root of the problem that it seeks to solve.

Imagine a patient with constant headaches. If a doctor just prescribes a painkiller, it may relieve the pain temporarily, but it won't be attacking the root of the problem. The sole mechanism of this problem could be an unbalanced diet, lack of sleep or even a vision problem that causes muscle tension in the head region.

By understanding the root of the problem, the doctor will be able to prescribe a specific treatment that will not only alleviate the pain, but will address the underlying cause. Likewise, by defining the problem's unique mechanism, it is possible to develop a single, effective solution that attacks that problem head-on.

For example, if the problem is the lack of efficiency in a production process in a factory, it is necessary to understand the reasons for this inefficiency. The unique mechanism could be a specific machine that constantly crashes, an employee that is not being properly trained, or a poorly structured process.

By understanding the unique mechanism of the problem, it is possible to develop a unique solution that attacks this problem head on. It could be a more modern machine that doesn't break down, specific training for the employee or a restructuring of the production process to make it more efficient.

In other words, the unique mechanism of the solution is created from the deep understanding of the unique mechanism of the problem. This is essential to developing an effective and unique solution that actually solves the problem and not just alleviates the symptoms.

Many companies make the mistake of developing solutions that don't address the unique mechanism of the problem, resulting in a solution that doesn't meet the customer's needs. It is therefore necessary to take a customer-oriented approach and deeply understand their needs and problems before developing a solution.

By understanding the root of the problem, it is also possible to develop solutions that not only attack the problem head on, but also solve underlying problems or secondary problems that arise from the main problem. This can be especially valuable for customers, who often experience multiple issues simultaneously.

Just look at these examples below:

Unique Mechanism of the Problem: The late-night snacking dilemma. Many people struggle to avoid late night snacking, which can derail their diet and weight loss goals.
Single Mechanism of Solution: Strategies to deal with hunger at night, such as having healthy snack options ready to eat, drinking water or teas, and setting specific meal times.

Unique Mechanism of the Problem: Sedentary lifestyle. With the modern lifestyle, many people spend most of their time sitting, which can lead to weight gain and health problems.
Unique Solution Mechanism: Encouragement of physical activity, including ideas for simple exercises that can be done at home or in the office, and strategies to make the daily routine more active.

Unique Mechanism of the Problem: The habit of eating out. Many people have difficulty maintaining a healthy diet when eating out, whether at restaurants or fast food outlets.

Single Mechanism of the Solution: Tips for choosing healthier options at restaurants, such as looking at the nutritional information on the menu, making simple dish modifications, and having a plan before you leave the house.

Unique Mechanism of the Problem: Hidden sugar in food. Food that looks healthy often contains large amounts of added sugar, which can sabotage a weight loss diet.

Single Solution Mechanism: Education on reading labels and identifying hidden sugars in seemingly healthy foods, as well as suggestions for healthier alternatives.

Unique Mechanism of the Problem: Lack of time to cook. Many people struggle to find time to cook healthy meals at home, which can lead to less healthy food choices.

Unique Mechanism of the Solution: Tips for preparing healthy meals in a short time, how to use pre-prepared ingredients and simple recipes, as well as suggestions for healthy meals to eat away from home.

Unique Mechanism of the Problem: Cravings for foods high in fat and carbohydrates. Many people struggle with cravings for foods that are unhealthy for a weight loss diet.
Single Mechanism of Solution: Strategies for dealing with food cravings, such as distracting yourself with other activities, making healthier choices, and allowing yourself a small amount of the desired food.

Now, see some real examples of how they were implemented in practice.

Used by the dietary supplement company BioFit. They use the solution's unique engine, featuring a product that contains a specific combination of probiotics that the company claims helps reduce inflammation, improve digestive health, and ultimately aid in weight loss.

Another interesting example is the unique mechanism of the problem used by the Whole30 weight loss program. They focus on identifying and eliminating inflammatory foods that may be causing weight gain and other health issues. They claim that by following their strict diet for 30 days, participants can heal their body and significantly improve their health.

Protein shake company IdealShape uses a unique engine of the solution, promoting shakes that help control appetite and replace unhealthy meals such as fast food. They claim that their shakes are an easy and convenient way to get the nutrients your body needs without going overboard on calories.

And the last single engine example of the solution is the gym apparel company Athleta. They focus on creating comfortable and stylish clothing for women who want to work out and feel great while doing it. The company claims its clothing is made with high-quality fabrics and designed to help women move freely without restrictions.

the perfect structure

In marketing, there are some frameworks and questions that can be useful to create a unique mechanism, such as:

Competitor analysis: It is important to understand what your competitors are offering and how they are positioning themselves in the market. This can help you identify opportunities to differentiate yourself and create a unique engine that meets customers' needs and wants differently than the competition.

Defining the target audience: It is essential to know your target audience and understand their needs, desires and purchasing behavior. Based on this information, it is possible to create a unique mechanism that meets the specific needs of this group of customers.

Identifying Unique Value: Ask yourself: What makes my product or service unique? What sets you apart from the competition? What makes it the best choice for my target audience? Identifying the unique value of your product or service can help create a strong unique engine.

Value proposition development: The value proposition is a clear and concise statement that communicates the unique value your product or service offers to customers. It's important to develop a strong and clear value proposition to help differentiate your brand and create a unique engine.

Testing and validation: After developing a unique mechanism, it is important to test and validate it with real customers. This can help identify strengths and weaknesses and refine the unique mechanism to make it more effective.

To find a unique way to make your product attractive, you can ask yourself the following questions:

Who is my target audience and what are their needs and wants?

What makes my product different from competing products and how can I highlight these differences?

What are my product's most valuable features and benefits, and how can I communicate these clearly and engagingly to my target audience?

What is the most appropriate tone and message for my brand and how can I convey it effectively?

How can I create a unique and enjoyable user experience around my product, be it through packaging, customer service or other initiatives?

By answering these questions you will be on the right path.

Conclusion

I hope it's clear how important a single engine can be to a brand's success in the marketplace. By creating a differential valued by customers and generating an emotional connection with the brand, it is possible to stand out from the competition and become a reference in the segment.

It is important to remember that creating the unique mechanism requires dedication and work, but the results can be very positive. By using this marketing strategy, the company can increase customer loyalty, brand engagement and, consequently, increase sales.

Therefore, if you are looking to stand out in the market and want to create a unique and admired brand, start thinking about how you can use the unique mechanism to your advantage. Identify what makes your brand special and value that differential. With hard work and dedication, I'm sure you can achieve the success you desire.

Who is Matheus Martins Soares?

 Matheus is an Ex-Military / Presidential Agent, graduated in Marketing since 2018 and specialist in copywriting. He has written for more than 27 different niches, showing his ability to adapt to different topics and audiences. Throughout his career, he has worked in large companies, such as the largest business magazine in the country and the largest marketing consultancy in Brazil. Contributed to the success of important campaigns, generating + 30mm in sales for its customers. Published over 100 books on Amazon and gained readers in over 10 different countries. An expert in StoryTelling and UX Writing, he also works behind the scenes as a GhostWriter, giving voice to other people's ideas and stories. His method is capable of writing a book in less than 24 hours.

With a strategic vision and knowledge in marketing, he helps companies, authors and literary projects to achieve success. He found himself in the world of marketing, writing and human behavior, his ability to adapt to different challenges is a differential that makes him stand out in his field.